GOLF ETIQUETTE
...AND USEFUL GOLF HABITS FOR KIDS

Golf etiquette and useful golf habits for kids.
Cooolz Ltd., 2022. 40 pages, illustrated.

ISBN 9798366489744

Editor   Cooolz Ltd.
Autor   Janina Spruza

Copyright © Cooolz Ltd.
Copyright © Use of characters, images, this book's idea or text without the author's permission is prohibited.

Dear friends!

Golf is an unusual game in that it has its own unique etiquette.

Etiquette is essentially a set of unofficial rules that golfers have been following for centuries.

It's based on simple principles: Be honest, respect yourself, and respect others. Simple as that!

This book will teach you not only about golf etiquette, but also about habits that you can apply in your everyday life.

Don't be late for your tee time, and don't delay other players during the round.

And please silence your cell phone!

Don't distract or otherwise interfere with a player as they prepare to swing. Just stay quiet and still until the ball has been hit, because you know how important it is to concentrate on each shot.

Always be honest.

Leave the ball where it lies, don't cheat, and don't let others cheat.

What kind of crazy person cries, complains, screams, argues, throws their golf bag, and pounds the grass with their club? Certainly not you.

After all, you are a future CHAMPION, and champions master themselves before they master the course.

To calm your nerves before a round, try listening to music, playing your favorite game, or reading a book.

Here's an exercise you can do when things just aren't going your way: Use your fingers to count to 10, closing each finger one by one as you count, then count back down from 10 to 1 as you open your fingers.

Don't stand or step on your fellow flight members' line when on the green. This is a very important rule, and violating it can upset your playing partners.

Respect and care for the course.

Use trash cans, replace your divots and repair pitch marks, rake bunkers, and let the greenkeepers pass so they can properly maintain the course for the benefit of all golfers.

Don't swing your club if someone is standing nearby.

It's very dangerous! Kindly ask them to move so you can swing safely.

When playing on the course, don't place your golf bag on tee boxes or greens – it is best to keep it just off to the side.

Once you finish your round or practice session, don't bring your golf bag into the clubhouse – put it next to the entrance or in a golf bag storage.

Wear golf attire and remove your hat when entering the clubhouse.

Don't drive your golf cart all over the course.

Stick to the paths.

What would happen if everyone started driving their golf carts around?

It would probably start to look like some sport other than golf.

Be honest on your scorecard. Compare your scores with those of your flight partners after each hole.

Any disagreements should be resolved immediately.

And don't be afraid to defend your score if someone else recorded it incorrectly. Stand up for yourself!

Always clean wet and dirty clubs before and after hitting a shot; use headcovers for your woods and putter to protect them from damage.

Keep your golf bag organized; and clean your shoes after each round.

Take some water and snacks with you to keep your energy up during the game. What and how much should you take?

If your answer was a few bottles of plain drinking water (no orange, blue, yellow, red, brown, or other colored drinks), a couple of bananas and nuts, then you are spot on!

Always stretch before starting a round or practice.

Your body must be warmed up to help you improve your game and avoid injury.

Remember, a practice round isn't a competition. It's an opportunity to get to know and explore the golf course.

Always keep this in mind: Use the practice round to study the course and consider possible scenarios, but don't calculate totals or compete with the other members in your flight. There's no such thing as a Practice-Round Champion.

Use an umbrella in rain or bright sunlight.

Get off the course or driving range whenever lightning is present. Lightning is extremely dangerous in open spaces and near trees, and is especially dangerous if you are holding a metal club.

Listen to and follow your coach's instructions.

You've learned about the basic golf rules and customs from this book, but show this book to your coach, too, and see if they have anything to add or highlight for you.

Enjoy the game.
Golf always presents an opportunity to enjoy the beauty of the course and have pleasant conversations.

Golf etiquette and useful golf habits for kids.
Cooolz Ltd., 2022. 40 pages, illustrated.
Author Janina Spruza

ISBN 9798366489744

Copyright © Cooolz Ltd.
Copyright © Use of characters, images, this book's idea or text without the author's permission is prohibited.

Printed in Great Britain
by Amazon